ALL PARIS

8th Edition, March 1990

I.S.B.N. 84-378-0776-X

Dep. Legal B. 9869-1990

A perspective of Paris. On the left, an elevated railway
station. In the centre of the photo, the Ecole Militaire, the
Eiffel Tower and Palais de Chaillot. In the background,
the tower blocks of La Défense.

PARIS: TWO THOUSAND YEARS OF HISTORY

The city of Paris was founded more than two thousand years ago, probably by the Gauls, who established a small settlement on the left bank of the Seine. Paris stands on several hills, some of which — such as Montmartre or Montparnasse — gave their names to popular, world-famous quarters.

Julius Caesar mentioned in his *Commentaries* the passage of Roman legions through *Lutetia,* the original nucleus of Paris. Due to the danger of barbarian incursions, the population moved to the Ile de la Cité, from whence the city began to expand on both banks of the Seine.

Legend has it that, after being converted in Athens by S Paul, S Denis was sent by Rome in the late Ist century to in turn convert the inhabitants of Paris; and that he founded the first church in the crypt of the old Carmelite monastery (Rue Denfert-Rochereau) and was later beheaded on Montmartre hill. Tradition also asserts that Geneviève (the name means "daughter of the heavens"), a humble shepherdess, presented herself before Bishop Marcel and obtained his permission to take the veil although she was only nine years old; and then persuaded the people of Lutetia not to abandon the city, assuring them that the Huns would not enter Paris. According to the legend, Geneviève's fervent prayers kept Attila and his mob at bay and saved the city from destruction.

Paris was first the residence of the Merovingian kings, then of the Carolingians. It became a real capital

Sunset over Notre-Dame.

One of the many artists enamoured of Paris.

Bouquinistes — second-hand book-stalls — on the embankments of the Seine.

Fantastic birds, monsters and devils in the Great Gallery of Notre-Dame dominating the Seine.

Notre-Dame from Quai de Montebello, on the bank of the Seine.

Place du Parvis; façade of Notre-Dame.

An old engraving of Notre-Dame.

Notre-Dame, on the Ile de la Cité. Further back, Square Jean XXIII.

Notre-Dame at night, from the Pont Saint-Michel.

Notre-Dame: the marvellous mediaeval stained-glass windows. ▷

Paris from the east side of Notre-Dame.

Square du Vert Galant, the western extreme of the lle de la Cité.

The banks of the Seine. ▷

Panorama of the Seine, Pont des Invalides, Pont Alexandre III, Grand Palais and Petit Palais.

Paris in the autumn, viewed from the Grand Palais.

when, in 987, Hugues Capet founded a new dynasty, giving rise to constant urban and cultural progress in the city. Paris thus became the true capital of France, and has retained this rank throughout history.

Around the year 1115, when Abélard was expounding his theories in the face of official orthodoxy, the physiognomy of Paris was already similar to its present appearance. King Philippe Auguste later consolidated the city's rôle as capital of France, providing it with an effective system of defence; and at the most vulnerable point he built the Louvre tower, "from whence all the fiefs of France were ordered." The University was founded in 1215 and its reputation spread rapidly throughout Europe. By the time Louis IX the Saint came to the throne, Paris was a flourishing city with splendid monuments.

In order to conserve the relics of the Passion that he had acquired, S Louis had the Sainte-Chapelle built

The Pont Alexandre III and the Hôtel des Invalides.

by the side of his palace; and his chaplain, Robert de Sorbon, set up a school for sixteen masters of art, which was called the Sorbonne.

Later, under the Valois monarchs, Paris lived some of the most sombre moments of its history; the revolt led by Etienne Marcel, the provost of Paris merchants, occurred in 1358. The marshals of Champagne and Normandy were executed and civil war broke out. Paris and the surrounding area were sacked; Marcel handed prisoners over to the English. The uprising concluded when Etienne Marcel was killed, near Porte Saint-Antoine, and the Dauphin

Charles, son of Jean the Good, returned from his captivity with the English: the inhabitants of the capital welcomed him joyfully. Charles V the Wise established order once more. But civil war broke out again, between the Armagnacs (supporters of the Duke of Orleans) and the Burgundians. The English took Paris and Henry VI was crowned king of France in Notre-Dame cathedral in 1430. Charles VII recaptured Paris seven years later but was unable to restore order: there were further bloody revolts which, added to devastating epidemics, produced many casualties. During this turbulent period (in the summer of 1431) a

The doorway of the Palais de Justice (Law Courts) and the Sainte-Chapelle.

Sainte-Chapelle: the interior.

The Conciergerie and Pont au Change.

The Clock Tower.

child destined to be France's first great modern poet was born in Paris: François Villon.

Internal strife continued to ravage the capital throughout the 16th century, culminating in the historic massacre of the Huguenots one sad night in 1572: August 24th, S Bartholomew's Day.

After the death of Henri III, assassinated by Jacques Clément, Paris underwent a siege lasting four years. The gates were finally opened to Henri IV, who was recognised as king of France after being converted to Catholicism. Henri IV (of Béarn) justified the repudiation of his religion with the historic phrase: ''Paris vaut bien une messe'' (''Paris is well worth a mass'').

△
The Arc de Triomphe du Carrousel. To the right, the Louvre (Marsan's wing).

◁ Maillol's statue in front of the Tuileries Garden.

Musée d'Orsay. ▷

The church of Saint-Germain-des-Prés, the oldest in Paris. Institut de France; the cupola of the Academy. Clubs, cafés and restaurants, meeting-places for friends, give life to the Saint-Germain-des-Prés quarter.

The Louvre pyramid; architect: M-Pei.

From this time onwards, the political and cultural influence of the French capital on the whole of Europe increased incessantly. The population reached 300,000 in the 17th century; by the early 18th century it was 500,000. At the end of that century Paris had the glory of being the centre of the Revolution that began with the capture of the Bastille on July 14th, 1789, and was to have far-reaching effects on the social and political schema of the modern world.

The fall of Louis XVI and the proclamation of the Republic, with its aftermath of terror, were followed by the Thermidor reaction. The Empire was established and Napoleon embellished the city unceasingly, raising monuments as famous as the Arc de Triomphe or the column in the Place Vendôme. Napoleon the Great, Charles X, Louis Philippe and the Second Republic fell one after another; in the reign of Napoleon III the urban structure of Paris was modernised under the supervision of Baron Haussmann, who had the markets of Les Halles built. The lay-out

The east façade of the Louvre: Perrault's colonnade.

The Louvre: the Victory of Samotharace.
(Photo: Musées Nationaux, Paris).

The Louvre: the Venus of Milo.
(Photo: Musées Nationaux, Paris).

The Louvre: Le Chancelier Nakht.
(Photo: Musées Nationaux, Paris).

The Louvre: The Vanquished Slave *by Michelangelo.*
(Photo: Musées Nationaux, Paris).

The Louvre: Millet's Les
glaneuses (The Gleaners).
(Photo: Musées Nationaux, Paris).

Oriental art: a bas-relief.

The Louvre: La liberté guidant le peuple, *by Delacroix.*
(Photo: Musées Nationaux, Paris).

of the main avenues was modified and the Woods of Boulogne and Vincennes were remodelled. The city's current elegant and fascinating appearance stems largely from the years of the Second Republic. When this latter collapsed as a result of the defeat at Sedan in 1870, the Commune was proclaimed and the city experienced dramatic times. Paris also underwent periods of great sadness in the first World War and, especially, during the German occupation of 1940-44. The city nevertheless recovered and once again became the beautiful capital that we see today.

VISITING PARIS

The Cité is the heart of Paris. Lying between two streams of the Seine, its present-day dimensions are practically the same as when its first inhabitants — as Maurice Garçon wrote — ''took refuge behind the reedbeds that lined its banks. It all started here. Originally comprising a handful of islets, the Cité became impregnable, and believed itself so; it struggled against all comers to preserve its independence, even protecting the riverside residents who gave it

The Louvre: David's
Coronation of
Napoleon I.
*(Photo: Musées Nationaux,
Paris).*

The Louvre: La mort
de Décus, *a tapestry
from Cluny.*
*(Photo: Musées Nationaux,
Paris).*

Avenue Winston Churchill; the Grand Palais.

The Petit Palais.

The Louvre: Leonardo da Vinci's La Joconde (Mona Lisa).
(Photo: Musées Nationaux, Paris).

Avenue des Champs-Elysées.

The Arc de Triomphe, in Place Charles de Gaulle.

High relief sculptured by Rude on the right-hand side of the Arc de Triomphe: "Departure of the Volunteers," popularly known as "La Marseillaise."

An effect of backlighting on the fountains in Place de la Concorde.

A winged horse on the Tuileries side of the Place de la Concorde. On the right, the Obelisk.

La Madeleine church.

Place de la Concorde by night; the Chambre des Députés (French Parliament) on the right.

Place Vendôme: a majestic ensemble of grand siècle (17th-century) architecture.

Paris: Hôtel de Ville (City Hall).

nothing in exchange. The Ile de la Cité is the mother but has been surrounded by its children. (...) Its silhouette evokes a past that is no more. (...) The Ile de la Cité was the largest island, its neighbours were the Ile Gourdaine, Ile des Juifs, Ile de la Treille and Ile du Moulin Buci. The Cité rapidly became a refuge when enemy incursions posed a threat. Monasteries were established around it: Sainte-Geneviève to the south, Saint-Germain-des-Prés to the west, Saint-Germain-l'Auxerrois to the north and Saint-Laurent to the east.''

The Cité was the centre of official activity from the 3rd century onwards. Notre-Dame cathedral stands on the site of an old Christian basilica, itself built on the foundations of a Roman temple. Bishop Maurice de Sully initiated the construction of the choir in 1163; the nave and aisles were built subsequently. The main front was finished around 1200 by Bishop Eudes de Sully; the belfries, in 1245. The chapels along the aisles and in the ambulatory were built later, whereas the façade of the north arm of the transept was completed in about 1250, and that of the south arm was begun some eight years later. The church was finished at the beginning of 1345.

In Robespierre's time Notre-Dame was devoted to the goddess Reason; and Napoleon was crowned there by Pope Pius VII in 1804. The silhouette of this cathedral is one of the most well-known images of Paris. The main front constitutes an admirable example of architectural balance and elegance of style: it comprises two galleries and is divided into three parts by columns. Outstanding elements in the ornamentation of this façade include the splendid 13th-century rose window, 10 m in diameter, the statues depicting kings of Israel and Judea, the beautiful double windows of the towers and the Gothic statues decorating the three doorways. The lateral belfries, 68 m high, are also remarkable: the *bourdon* (great bell), weighing 13 tonnes, is in one of them. The spire reaches a height of 96 m above ground-level.

Place de l'Opéra.

The Paris Opera (National Academy of Music).

Magnificent interior furnishings of the Opera.

Le Dôme church, one of the greatest masterpieces of Louis XIV's century.

Les Invalides: overall view from the north side.

Napoleon's tomb.

The Champ-de-Mars from the Trocadéro gardens.

The Eiffel Tower; gilded bronze statues on the terrace of the Palais du Trocadéro.

Overall view of the Palais du Trocadéro, gardens and the play of the fountains; in the background, Place du Trocadéro.

*Luxembourg palace
and gardens.*

Jardin du Luxembourg with the Pantheon in the background.

The interior of Notre-Dame resembles the shape of an inverted boat. It is 35 m high, 130 m long and 48 m wide, with a capacity for 9,000 people. Special mention is due to the choir, with magnificent 17th-century wooden panelling, made up of 78 artistic choir-stalls. The calottes of deceased cardinals, whose tombs are in the retrochoir, hang from the roof vaults. The Cathedral Treasure, made up of relics and of precious articles for the liturgy, is kept in the Chapter Sacristy, to the right of the choir.

By taking the Pont Saint-Louis one can cross from the Cité to the Ile Saint-Louis, where the monuments include the Archbishops' Palace (18th-century), Saint-Louis church (17th-century, with sumptuous decoration inside) and the Hôtel Lambert, where Voltaire was the guest of the Marquise de Châtelet. Further towards Quai de Béthune, the visitor will find the Hôtel du Duc de Richelieu, the Mieckiewicz Museum and the Polish Library. A statue of S Geneviève, patron saint of Paris — by Landowski — stands to the left of the Pont de la Tournette. Having crossed the Seine, one reaches the Hôtel de

The fountain in Place Edmond Rostand. The Pantheon is at the end of Rue Soufflot.

Quai de la Mégisserie, with the florists' stalls.

Under the arcades of Place des Vosges.

The Saint-Michel quarter: an English bookshop, near the Petit Pont.

Sorbonne church in Place de la Sorbonne.

The flower-
market at
Quai aux
Fleurs.

Hôtel de Sens, one of the three great private residences of the Middle Ages in Paris.

Place des Vosges, the oldest monumental square in Paris. ▷
Hôtel de Rohan-Soubise. Place des Vosges. ▷

Ville (City Hall), located in the time-honoured Place de la Grève, scene of important historical events, where the guillotine was first installed. This building displays a façade in the French Renaissance style, a faithful reproduction of the one burnt down in 1871 in the course of the disturbances that marked the Revolution of the Commune. The Hôtel de Ville houses an important museum of modern painting and sculpture. The Hall of Caryatids, Science Room, Arts Room, Lobau Gallery and the Council Chamber are all interesting. There is a statue of Etienne Marcel not far from the building.

The Louvre is a monument closely linked to the history of France. This famous building houses one of the most important museums in the world. The colonnade of the façade, in the classical style, was designed by Claude Perrault, and built from 1667 to 1673. It comprises three sections, the colonnade is formed by tall pairs of columns standing on a high plinth with windows. The main entrance of the Museum is in the centre of the Pavillon Denon, which features a cupola on a quadrangular base, a portico with archways and a terrace adorned with statues of famous personages. The courtyard known as the Cour Carrée, in the Renaissance style, belongs to the Old Louvre, a fortress converted into a royal palace by Charles V. The construction of this part of the building began in the reign of François I and was concluded in 1660.

Tour Saint-Jacques, the bell-tower of the church of Saint-Jacques-la-Boucherie at the time of François I.

The New Louvre, on either side of the Arc du Triomphe du Carrousel, was built by Visconti and Lefuel in 1852. The triumphal arch is surmounted by a bronze quadriga commemorating Napoleon's victories of 1805.

Of all the valuable works of art gathered together in the Louvre, we would mention the *Venus of Milo,* a Greek statue discovered in 1820 on the island of the same name; the *Victory of Samothrace,* found on the island of Samothrace in 1863; and the *Mona Lisa (La Joconde),* Leonardo da Vinci's masterpiece. Also *La Liberté guidant le peuple,* a famous painting by Delacroix; *The Coronation of Napoleon I,* painted by Jacques Louis David; and the extraordinary collections of Persian, Egyptian, Greek and Mesopotamian art.

Other important museums in Paris include the Jeu de Paume and the Orangerie, in which one can admire the essential works of Manet, Pissarro, Toulouse-Lautrec, Cézanne, Gauguin, Van Gogh and other masters of 19th-century painting.

The Place de la Concorde, previously also named after Louis XV and the Revolution, is nearby; by virtue of its spacious dimensions and balanced architecture it is considered to be the most beautiful, elegant square in the world. In the centre stands an obelisk that Ramses II raised in front of the temple at Luxor, a gift from Egypt to King Louis Philippe in 1831. The square is adorned by eight statues representing the major cities of France, and by splendid fountains designed by Hittorf, which are illuminated at night.

The Pont de la Concorde, to the south of the square, is 36 m long and spans the Seine opposite the Chamber of Deputies. The statue of King Albert I of Belgium faces west; next to it is the beginning of the famous, dazzling Avenue des Champs-Elysées, with "Marly's Horses," a statue by Guillaume Coustou. This is the most lavish avenue in Paris, with its flowerbeds, luxury restaurants, theatres, department stores; and its elegant perspective.

Place de la République.

Place du Châtelet with the fountain — "Fontaine du Palmier" — commemorating the triumphs of Napoleon I.

Place de la Nation. In the centre, "the Triumph of the Republic"

Place de la Bastille and the "July Column," raised in memory of the Parisians killed during the troubled days of July 1830.

The Place de l'Etoile and the Arc de Triomphe are at the other end of the Champs-Elysées; the Arch, one of the most popular monuments in Paris, was begun under Chalgrin's supervision in 1806, and concluded in 1836. Napoleon had it built as a tribute to his victorious troops: it measures 50 m high by 45 m wide. The arch displays large bas-reliefs; special mention is due to the one facing the Champs-Elysées — by François Rude, entitled "La Marseillaise" — depicting the departure of volunteers in 1792.

Place Daumesnil.

Sacré-Coeur Basilica, on Montmartre hill.

Sacré-Coeur.

Inside the Basilica.

Another important hub of Paris is the semicircular Place du Trocadéro. The Palais de Chaillot is here, housing the Museums of Man, French Monuments, French Folklore and the Musée de la Marine. The monuments to Maréchal Foch and Benjamin Franklin are next to the Palais de Chaillot. The Eiffel Tower is also nearby: 300 m high, it was constructed of 15,000 metal sections joined by 2,500,000 rivets. Gustave Eiffel, the engineer, built it for the 1889 *Exposition Universelle* (World Fair). From the circular gallery at the top one can enjoy splendid views of the city and surrounding area. The Champ de Mars, at the foot of the Eiffel Tower, was formerly the scene of military manoeuvres. Further back, behind the statue of Maréchal Joffre, is the Ecole Militare (built by Gabriel

in 1752); and behind that, the Palais de l'UNESCO. The UNESCO building was designed by a Frenchman, a North American and an Italian: Zehrfus, Breuer and Nervi, respectively. The interior is embellished by Picasso's fresco entitled *The Fall of Icarus,* sculptures by Henry Moore, a mobile by Calder, ceramics by Miró and Artigas, and paintings by Arp, Afro, Appel and Malta.

The Palais de l'Elysée, the President of the Republic's residence, stands to the right of the elegant Faubourg Saint-Honoré. The Ministry of the Interior is in Place Beauvau.

The Vendôme Column is another important Parisian monument, in the centre of Place Vendôme. It is adorned by 400 reliefs, arranged in a spiral, relating

Napoleon's campaign of 1805; and surmounted by a statue of the Emperor. The column was constructed in 1806, using the bronze from 1,200 cannons captured by French troops at the Battle of Austerlitz. There is a statue of Joan of Arc in Rue des Pyramides, on the spot where the heroine fell wounded during the siege of Paris.

The popular area occupied by the main boulevards — Montmartre, des Italiens, des Capucines and de la Madeleine — is a fascinating hive of activity, always very busy, with its cafés, cinemas and luxury shops. The Place de l'Opéra is the nerve-centre of the boulevards, and the Opera (or National Academy of Music and Dance), built in the Second Empire style

Montmartre, a celebrated centre of bohemian life.

The picturesque Place du Tertre.

Saint-Martin canal.

The steps ascending the Butte (hill) of Montmartre.

by Charles Garnier in 1861, is there; its façade is adorned by Corinthian columns and groups of statues. The Opera occupies an area of 11,000 square metres and is considered to be the largest in the world; it also houses the Museums of Theatre and Music.

Montmartre is one of the most universally famous quarters of Paris. There are numerous cabarets, night-clubs, cinemas and theatres in this area. Sacré-Coeur Basilica, on the top of Montmartre hill, is 100 m long by 50 m wide; the cupola measures 83 m and the belfry, 94 m — the latter contains "la Savoyarde," one of the largest bells in the world, weighing 22 tonnes. There is a fascinating panorama of Paris to be enjoyed from the terrace in front of the church, one can easily make out many of the most important monuments in the city.

The quarter of Les Halles Centrales (the former Central Market) and the area around Place de la République are also very active. Special mention is due, by

Montmartre. The Consulate, a vestige of the historic free Commune of Montmartre. Pigalle: Place Blanche at night and the illuminated sails of the Moulin Rouge. Metro entrance dating from the beginning of the century ("noodle" style), designed by Guimard.

*Tour Montparnasse
and the Shopping
Centre.*

*The Paris International
Centre: Congress Hall.*

*Headquarters of
Radio-France. Pont de
Grenelle and the
Statue of Liberty (a
scale reproduction of
Bartholdi's, in New
York).*

Forum des Halles.

*The R.E.R. (Résau
Express Régional —
Express Network).*

The Défense, the towers and the "Grande Arche".

The Centre Georges Pompidou, on the Beaubourg plateau.

Front de Seine, an audacious housing development.

virtue of their historical interest, to the Temple area (the Tour du Temple, demolished in 1811, was Louis XVI's prison until he was taken to the guillotine); and to Rue des Archives and Rue des Francs-Bourgeois — the "Palace of National Archives" is situated at their intersection, and the Museum of Contemporary History is near at hand. Also the Place des Vosges — the houses here were inhabited by the high society of Paris from the time of Henri IV to the 17th century — and the Place de la Bastille, where the famous fortress used to stand. The Colonne de Juillet ("July Column") now stands in the centre of the square, surmounted by the Spirit of Liberty, a sculpture commemorating the Revolution of July 1830.

The enchanting Quartier Latin — Latin Quarter — is possibly the most popular part of Paris among foreign visitors. Thousands and thousands of students from many different countries attend the classes given in the diverse faculties, lycées and schools that operate here; the area is also very popular with writers and artists. There are abundant restaurants of all kinds, well-stocked bookshops, welcoming cafés, cinemas... The *bouquinistes* or second-hand bookstalls on the banks of the Seine are particularly interesting: a fascinating, typical image of Paris. The prestigious University of Paris has its base in Place de la Sorbonne.

The Panthéon, on the top of Montagne Sainte-Geneviève, was built in 1757 according to plans by Soufflot and displays a triangular pediment and a cupola 83 m high. Voltaire, Victor Hugo, Emile Zola and other illustrious Frenchmen are buried here. The

Jeune fille en fleur, *by Rodin.*

The Rodin Museum.

Jardins du Luxembourg —the students' gardens — are particularly attractive; they cover an area of some 23 hectares. Opposite the gardens stands the Palais du Luxembourg, seat of the Senate, built in 1615 as a residence for Queen Mary de Medici. Nearby, one can visit Saint-Sulpice church (with valuable paintings and sculptures in the interior) and the Place de Saint-Germain-des-Prés, where the church features an 11th-century tower, the oldest in the whole city.

The Hôtel des Invalides is also of great interest; by the entrance to this monument there are many cannons captured from the enemy in different periods. The Army Museum is installed here; and in Saint-Louis church there is a chapel conserving numerous mementoes of Napoleon. The dome of Les Invalides, 105 m high, is in Place Vauban, adjacent to the church, and shelters Napoleon I's tomb.

Vincennes, with its celebrated mediaeval castle, is in the eastern part of Paris, while the Bois de Boulogne, the Parisians' garden, is to the west of the city, with two main entrances: Porte Maillot and Porte Dauphine.

Le Penseur
(The
Thinker), *by
Rodin.*

Roissy-en-France, the major Paris airport.

Forum des Halles, by the architects Vasconi and Pencreac'h. Place Basse and, in the middle, sculpture by Julio Silva.

The site of Sciences and Industry at La Villette — La Géode.

Paris-Bercy Omnisports Palace — Architects: Andrault and Parat.

Palace of Versailles: the "royal courtyard."

VERSAILLES

Louis XIII was a keen hunter and in Val de Galie, Versailles, he discovered an ideal place for a hunting lodge; the accommodation for the hunter king was begun in 1623. The site was, however, so charming, and so pleased Louis XIII, that in 1631 he had Le Roy build a real château. Louis XIV enlarged and embellished Versailles and commissioned the three wings appended to the original palace. The landscape-gardener Le Nôtre, Le Brun the painter, Le Vau and François Mansart (architects), among others, contributed to the splendour of Versailles.

Versailles is crossed by three major avenues, converging on the great esplanade of the Place des Armes (parade ground), the beginning of the gardens that afford entrance to the palace. The most remarkable parts of the interior are the royal chapel, dedicated to S Louis — this palace chapel is made up of two storeys, with paintings on the ceiling that contrast

The Orangery, Hameau ("Hamlet") de Marie-Antoinette, and the Temple of Love.

The "parterres d'eau" and, in the foreground, "Le Rhône."

with the white and gold tones predominating in the chapel; the Salon d'Hercule ("Hercules' Room"), with walls built of marble of different colours, and the ceiling painted by Le Moyne; the Salon de Vénus, where the ceiling is adorned with a painting by R. A. Houasse entitled *Vénus assujetissant à son empire les divinités et les puissances;* the Salon de Diane, decorated by Gabriel Blanchard; and the Salon de Mars, featuring two beautiful tapestries, canvases by Rigaud and Van Loo, and ceiling paintings by Audran, Jouvenet and Houasse. Similarly, the Galerie des Glaces ("Hall of Mirrors"), with the ceiling decorated by Le Brun, where important receptions and celebrations are held; the King's Chamber, retaining magnificent tapestries from Les Gobelins, designed by Le Brun, and a bust of Louis XIV by Coysevox; the Queen's Chamber, occupied first by Marie-Thérèse and later by Marie-Antoinette, displaying medallions decorated by Boucher, beautiful tapestries and Schwerdfegger's jewel case adorned with Sèvres

The Hall of Mirrors.
(Photo: Musées Nationaux, Paris).

porcelain and miniatures; the Queen's inner chambers; Louis XV's Chamber; and the theatre.

Versailles has been the scene of important historical events. As well as the palace, the gardens created by Le Nôtre are of great interest. They are entirely dedicated to Apollo, and structured around two main axes, one orientated towards the west, the other running north-south. The first-mentioned descends from the centre of the palace to the Grand Canal, 1,650 m long by 62 m wide. The second avenue crosses the first Parterre d'Eau (pool), runs parallel to the façade of the château, and then slopes down to the Cent Marches ("Hundred Steps," two stairways separated by Mansart's orangery) and the Lake of the Swiss. The gardens are adorned by statues from the time of Louis XIV, by the fountains of Ceres, Flora and the Obelisk, and the enormous basin of Enceladus: a realm of extraordinary, indescribable beauty.

One should not neglect also to visit the Grand Trianon and the Petit Trianon, built near the Grand Canal by Louis XIV, Louis XV and Louis XVI.

The Gallery of Battles.
(Photo: Musées Nationaux, Paris).

Apollon servi par les Nymphes, *by Girardon and Regnaudin.*
(Photo: Musées Nationaux, Paris).

The Champ-de-Mars and the Eiffel Tower at night.

Collection ALL EUROPE

	Spanish	French	English	German	Italian	Catalan	Dutch	Swedish	Portuguese	Japanese	Finnish
1 ANDORRA	•	•	•	•	•	•					
2 LISBON	•	•	•	•					•		
3 LONDON	•	•	•	•	•					•	
4 BRUGES	•	•	•	•			•				
5 PARIS	•	•	•	•	•					•	
6 MONACO	•	•	•	•	•						
7 VIENNA	•	•	•	•	•			•		•	
8 NICE	•	•	•	•	•						
9 CANNES	•	•	•	•							
10 ROUSSILLON	•	•	•	•			•				
11 VERDUN	•	•	•	•			•				
12 THE TOWER OF LONDON	•	•	•	•							
13 ANTWERP	•	•	•	•			•				
14 WESTMINSTER ABBEY	•	•	•	•							
15 THE SPANISH RIDING SCHOOL IN VIENNA	•	•	•	•	•						
16 FATIMA	•	•	•	•	•				•		
17 WINDSOR CASTLE	•	•	•	•	•					•	
18 THE OPAL COAST		•	•								
19 COTE D'AZUR	•	•	•	•	•						
20 AUSTRIA		•	•	•	•						
21 LOURDES	•	•	•	•							
22 BRUSSELS	•	•	•	•	•		•				
23 SCHÖNBRUNN PALACE	•	•	•	•	•						
24 ROUTE OF PORT WINE	•	•	•	•	•				•		
25 CYPRUS		•	•	•				•			
26 HOFBURG PALACE	•	•	•	•	•						
27 ALSACE	•	•	•	•	•		•				
28 RHODES		•	•	•							
29 BERLIN	•	•	•	•							
30 CORFU		•	•	•							
31 MALTA		•	•	•							
32 PERPIGNAN		•									
33 STRASBOURG	•	•	•	•							
34 MADEIRA	•	•	•	•							
35 CERDAGNE - CAPCIR		•				•					

Collection ART IN SPAIN

	Spanish	French	English	German	Italian	Catalan	Dutch	Swedish	Portuguese	Japanese	Finnish
1 PALAU DE LA MUSICA CATALANA (Catalan Palace of Music)	•	•	•	•		•					
2 GAUDI	•	•	•	•	•					•	
3 PRADO MUSEUM I (Spanish Painting)	•	•	•	•	•					•	
4 PRADO MUSEUM II (Foreign Painting)	•	•	•								
5 MONASTERY OF GUADALUPE	•										
6 THE CASTLE OF XAVIER	•	•	•	•							
7 THE FINE ARTS MUSEUM OF SEVILLE	•	•	•	•							
8 SPANISH CASTLES	•	•	•								
9 THE CATHEDRALS OF SPAIN	•	•	•								
10 THE CATHEDRAL OF GERONA	•										
11 GRAN TEATRE DEL LICEU DE BARCELONA (The Great Opera House)	•	•	•	•	•	•					
12 THE ROMANESQUE STYLE IN CATALONIA	•	•	•	•							
13 LA RIOJA: ART TREASURES AND WINE-GROWING RESOURCES	•	•	•								
14 PICASSO	•	•	•								
15 REALES ALCAZARES (ROYAL PALACE OF SEVILLE)	•	•	•	•							
16 MADRID'S ROYAL PALACE	•	•	•	•							
17 ROYAL MONASTERY OF EL ESCORIAL	•	•	•	•							
18 THE WINES OF CATALONIA	•										
19 THE ALHAMBRA AND THE GENERALIFE	•	•	•	•	•						
20 GRANADA AND THE ALHAMBRA (ARAB AND MAURESQUE MONUMENTS OF CORDOVA, SEVILLE AND GRANADA)	•										
21 ROYAL ESTATE OF ARANJUEZ	•	•	•	•							
22 ROYAL ESTATE OF EL PARDO	•	•	•								
23 ROYAL HOUSES	•	•	•								
24 ROYAL PALACE OF SAN ILDEFONSO	•	•	•								
25 HOLY CROSS OF THE VALLE DE LOS CAIDOS	•	•	•								
26 OUR LADY OF THE PILLAR OF SARAGOSSA	•	•	•								

Collection ALL SPAIN

	Spanish	French	English	German	Italian	Catalan	Dutch	Swedish	Portuguese	Japanese	Finnish
1 ALL MADRID	•	•	•	•	•					•	
2 ALL BARCELONA	•	•	•	•	•	•					
3 ALL SEVILLE	•	•	•	•	•					•	
4 ALL MAJORCA	•	•	•	•	•		•				
5 ALL THE COSTA BRAVA	•	•	•	•	•						
6 ALL MALAGA and the Costa del Sol	•	•	•	•	•		•				
7 ALL THE CANARY ISLANDS, Gran Canaria, Lanzarote and Fuerteventura	•	•	•	•	•		•	•			
8 ALL CORDOBA	•	•	•	•	•					•	
9 ALL GRANADA	•	•	•	•	•		•			•	
10 ALL VALENCIA	•	•	•	•	•						
11 ALL TOLEDO	•	•	•	•	•					•	
12 ALL SANTIAGO	•	•	•	•	•						
13 ALL IBIZA and Formentera	•	•	•	•	•						
14 ALL CADIZ and the Costa de la Luz	•	•	•	•	•						
15 ALL MONTSERRAT	•	•	•	•	•	•					
16 ALL SANTANDER and Cantabria	•	•	•	•							
17 ALL THE CANARY ISLANDS II, Tenerife, La Palma, Gomera, Hierro	•	•	•	•	•		•	•			•
18 ALL ZAMORA	•	•	•	•							
19 ALL PALENCIA	•	•	•	•							
20 ALL BURGOS, Covarrubias and Santo Domingo de Silos	•	•	•	•	•						
21 ALL ALICANTE and the Costa Blanca	•	•	•	•	•		•				
22 ALL NAVARRA	•	•	•	•							
23 ALL LERIDA, Province and Pyrenees	•	•	•	•	•						
24 ALL SEGOVIA and Province	•	•	•	•	•						
25 ALL SARAGOSSA and Province	•	•	•	•							
26 ALL SALAMANCA and Province	•	•	•	•					•		
27 ALL AVILA and Province	•	•	•	•							
28 ALL MINORCA	•	•	•	•							
29 ALL SAN SEBASTIAN and Guipúzcoa	•										
30 ALL ASTURIAS	•	•	•	•							
31 ALL LA CORUNNA and the Rías Altas	•	•	•	•							
32 ALL TARRAGONA and Province	•	•	•	•							
33 ALL MURCIA and Province	•	•	•	•							
34 ALL VALLADOLID and Province	•	•	•	•							
35 ALL GIRONA and Province	•	•	•	•							
36 ALL HUESCA and Province	•	•									
37 ALL JAEN and Province	•	•	•	•							
38 ALL ALMERIA and Province	•	•	•	•							
39 ALL CASTELLON and the Costa del Azahar	•	•	•	•							
40 ALL CUENCA and Province	•	•	•	•							
41 ALL LEON and Province	•	•	•	•							
42 ALL PONTEVEDRA, VIGO and the Rías Bajas	•	•	•	•							
43 ALL RONDA	•	•	•	•	•						
44 ALL SORIA	•		•								
45 ALL HUELVA	•	•	•								
46 ALL EXTREMADURA	•										
47 ALL GALICIA	•	•	•	•							
48 ALL ANDALUSIA	•	•	•	•	•						
49 ALL CATALONIA	•	•	•	•	•	•					
50 ALL LA RIOJA	•	•	•	•	•						

Collection ALL AMERICA

	Spanish	French	English	German	Italian	Catalan	Dutch	Swedish	Portuguese	Japanese	Finnish
1 PUERTO RICO	•		•								
2 SANTO DOMINGO	•		•								
3 QUEBEC		•	•								
4 COSTA RICA	•		•								

Collection ALL AFRICA

	Spanish	French	English	German	Italian	Catalan	Dutch	Swedish	Portuguese	Japanese	Finnish
1 MOROCCO	•	•	•	•	•						
2 THE SOUTH OF MOROCCO	•	•	•	•	•						
3 TUNISIA		•	•								

The printing of this book was completed
in the workshops of
FISA - ESCUDO DE ORO, S.A.
Palaudarias, 26 - Barcelona (Spain)